# ADVANCED PATTERN RECOGNITION

AN ART OF JOURNALING BONUS GUIDE

THE JOURNALING MASTERY SERIES: THEORY
AND PRACTICE
BOOK 4

## RICHARD FRENCH

# Indie Pen Press

TURNING DREAMS INTO BESTSELLERS

Indie Pen Press
600 1st Ave Ste 330 PMB 582144
Seattle, Washington 98104-2246
IndiePenPress.com

First Edition December 2024

Paperback ISBN: 979-8-9917570-9-6

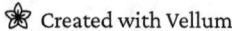 Created with Vellum

# ONE
# BEYOND BASIC PATTERNS

E mma stared at her collection of journals, colored tabs marking different types of entries. Something had been nagging at her lately—a sense that beneath the obvious patterns she'd been tracking, deeper connections waited to be discovered. She opened her latest journal to an entry from three months ago:

*"Another presentation derailed by questions. Heart racing, palms sweaty. Just like last time. Just like every time."*

Next to it, she'd noted a pattern: "Public speaking anxiety." But today, as she reviewed more entries, she noticed something new. Each challenging presentation had been preceded by late-night preparation and skipped morning meditation. The anxiety wasn't just about public speaking—it was part of a larger pattern involving preparation habits, self-care routines, and professional confidence.

"It's not just one pattern," Emma whispered, reaching for a fresh page. "It's a pattern of patterns."

# THE EVOLUTION OF PATTERN RECOGNITION

When we first learn to recognize patterns in our journaling practice, we typically start with obvious connections: emotional responses to specific situations, recurring behaviors, or regular reactions. These surface patterns are valuable, but they're just the beginning.

Think of patterns like a forest. At first glance, you see trees. Look closer, and you notice different species. Spend more time observing, and you begin to understand how these trees interact with each other, with the soil, and with the weather systems above them. You discover that what appeared to be individual trees are actually part of a vast, interconnected ecosystem.

James discovered this while reviewing his journals from the past year. He'd initially identified what seemed like separate patterns:

- Productivity drops on Wednesdays
- Tension with his team during project deadlines
- Creative blocks in the afternoon
- Increased coffee consumption mid-week

But as he mapped these patterns together, a meta-pattern emerged. His Wednesday productivity dips weren't isolated events—they were part of an energy management pattern that affected his leadership style, creative capacity, and physical habits. This discovery led him to a deeper understanding of his weekly rhythms and how they influenced multiple areas of his life.

## THE META-PATTERN FRAMEWORK

Let's explore how James used the first advanced template to uncover this meta-pattern:

## PATTERN ECOSYSTEM MAP

```
Central Pattern: Wednesday Energy Dip

Connected Patterns:
1. Physical
   - Increased caffeine intake
   - Disrupted sleep on Tuesday nights
   - Afternoon headaches

2. Professional
   - Shorter patience with the team
   - Decreased creative output
   - Delayed decision-making

3. Environmental
   - Cluttered desk by Wednesday
   - Unanswered emails accumulating
   - Missed morning preparation time

Intersection Points:
- Tuesday evening preparation affects Wednesday morning energy
- Coffee increase impacts afternoon mood
- Desk clutter influences creative blocks
```

## EXERCISE: CREATING YOUR FIRST PATTERN ECOSYSTEM MAP

1. Choose a recurring pattern you've noticed
2. List all connected behaviors, emotions, and situations
3. Draw lines between related elements
4. Note the timing of connections
5. Identify potential influence points

*James's Implementation:* He spread his journal entries across his desk, with different colored sticky notes marking each type of pattern. As he connected them with drawn lines, the relationships became clear. His Wednesday energy dip wasn't the problem—it was a signal of a larger pattern involving preparation habits, energy management, and leadership style.

This understanding led to a series of small but powerful changes:

1. Moving team meetings to Thursday
2. Establishing Tuesday evening planning
3. Creating Wednesday morning space

The result wasn't just improved Wednesdays—the entire week's rhythm shifted, demonstrating how understanding meta-patterns can create systemic change.

## WHY ADVANCED PATTERN RECOGNITION MATTERS

Sarah sat in her favorite coffee shop, three journals spread before her. The morning sun cast shadows across pages filled with her familiar handwriting. She'd been tracking her "productivity pattern" for months, noting when she worked best, what disrupted her flow, and how different environments affected her output. But today, something different caught her attention.

"It's not just about productivity," she murmured, drawing a fresh diagram in her notebook. Her eyes moved between entries from different months:

*March 15: "Incredible flow state this morning. Three hours of uninterrupted writing. Feeling energized and clear."*

*April 3: "Another powerful morning session. Something about the quiet, the routine, the certainty of it all."*
*May 21: "Can't focus. Everything feels off. Skipped morning routine, rushed to the meeting."*

What she'd labeled as a "productivity pattern" was actually an intersection point of multiple patterns:

## PATTERN INTERSECTION MAP

```
Core Pattern: Morning Productivity

Intersecting Patterns:
1. Environmental
   └ Physical Space
      ├ Light quality
      ├ Ambient noise
      └ Temperature

2. Behavioral
   └ Morning Routine
      ├ Wake-up time
      ├ Exercise
      └ Meditation

3. Physiological
   └ Energy Levels
      ├ Sleep Quality
      ├ Nutrition
      └ Hydration

4. Psychological
   └ Mental State
      ├ Preparation
      ├ Clarity
      └ Purpose
```

## EXERCISE: PATTERN INTERSECTION ANALYSIS

1. Select a primary pattern you've identified.

2. Create four quadrants: Environmental, Behavioral, Physiological, and Psychological.
3. Map related elements in each quadrant
4. Draw connection lines between influences.
5. Note the strength of connections (strong, moderate, weak).

*Sarah's Implementation:* She took a fresh page and drew the quadrants. As she mapped each element, connections emerged that she hadn't noticed before. Her most productive mornings weren't just about having a quiet space or following a routine —they emerged from the harmony of multiple patterns working together.

Next to her map, she started a new entry:

*"I'm seeing it now. My best work doesn't come from forcing productivity. It emerges from the intersection of well-maintained patterns. When my environment supports my behavior and my physical needs align with my mental state, flow happens naturally. It's not about optimizing one pattern; it's about orchestrating many."*

## PATTERN COMPOUNDS

Understanding pattern compounds—how patterns build upon and influence each other—reveals opportunities for profound change. Tom discovered this while reviewing his "relationship patterns" journal entries. He'd initially focused on communication styles and conflict triggers, but deeper analysis revealed a compound pattern:

## PATTERN COMPOUND TEMPLATE

```
Base Pattern: Communication Style
↓
Influencing Pattern: Energy Management
↓
Behavioral Pattern: Response to Stress
↓
Environmental Pattern: Work Pressure
↓
Compound Effect: Relationship Dynamics
```

## EXERCISE: IDENTIFYING PATTERN COMPOUNDS

1. Choose a significant pattern in your life.
2. List all patterns that influence it.
3. Map the flow of influence.
4. Note amplification points.
5. Identify intervention opportunities.

*Tom's Implementation:* Opening to a clean page, he created columns for each pattern layer. As he filled them in, he saw how work stress affected his energy, which influenced his communication, ultimately impacting his relationships. This wasn't just about "improving communication" but about understanding and managing the entire pattern compound.

Through this advanced pattern recognition, Tom could see why previous attempts to "communicate better" had limited success. He needed to address the entire compound, not just its surface manifestation.

# TWO
# THE META-PATTERN
# FRAMEWORK

Amanda closed her laptop, rubbing her temples. After months of journaling about her "procrastination pattern," something wasn't adding up. She spread her journals across her dining room table with different-colored high-lighters in hand: yellow for procrastination incidents, b, green for successful task completion, blue for emotional states, and pink for environmental factors.

As patterns emerged under the colored ink, her eyes widened. "It's not procrastination," she whispered. "It's a protection pattern."

## UNDERSTANDING PATTERN LAYERS

Think of pattern layers like an archaeological dig. Surface patterns are easily visible, but each layer we uncover reveals deeper truths about our behaviors, emotions, and core motivations. Let's follow Amanda's discovery process:

## PATTERN LAYER ANALYSIS TEMPLATE

```
Surface Layer: Procrastination
└ Observable Behavior
   ├ Delayed project starts
   ├ Last-minute rushes
   └ Task avoidance

Behavioral Layer: Protection Mechanisms
└ Action Patterns
   ├ Perfectionism
   ├ Over-preparation
   └ Fear of judgment

Emotional Layer: Core Feelings
└ Internal Experience
   ├ Anxiety about failure
   ├ Fear of Success
   └ Need for control

Core Layer: Fundamental Needs
└ Basic Drivers
   ├ Safety
   ├ Validation
   └ Self-worth

Meta-Pattern: Self-Protection System
```

## EXERCISE: LAYER MAPPING

1. Choose a persistent pattern
2. Create your layer template
3. Start at the surface
4. Dig deeper with each layer
5. Connect the layers

*Amanda's Implementation:* She opened to a fresh page, drawing horizontal lines to create layers. At the top, she listed procrastination behaviors. But as she worked downward, something shifted. Her hand trembled slightly as she wrote:

*"It's not that I can't start—it's that I'm trying to protect myself from potential failure. Each delay is a shield, and each postponement is a safety net. The procrastination isn't the pattern; it's the symptom of a deeper protection pattern."*

## PATTERN INTERSECTIONS

As Amanda dug deeper, she noticed how her protection pattern intersected with other life areas. She created an intersection map:

## PATTERN INTERSECTION TEMPLATE

```
Central Pattern: Self-Protection
↓
Professional Life
├─ Delayed project initiatives
├─ Over-preparation for meetings
└─ Hesitation in sharing ideas

Personal Life
├─ Postponed dating
├─ Limited social commitments
└─ Controlled environments

Creative Expression
├─ Unshared writing
├─ "Perfect" conditions needed
└─ Critical inner voice

Health & Wellness
├─ Safe exercise choices
├─ Familiar routines only
└─ Risk avoidance
```

*Amanda's Journal Entry: "Seeing these intersections is like finding hidden doorways in a familiar house. Each area of my life bears the fingerprint of this protection pattern. It's not just about work deadlines but how I approach life itself. The pattern ripples outward, touching everything."*

## PATTERN EVOLUTION TRACKING

Understanding how patterns evolve reveals opportunities for transformation. Amanda began tracking her protection pattern's evolution:

## PATTERN EVOLUTION TEMPLATE

```
Pattern Name: Self-Protection Through Delay
Current Stage: Awareness & Transformation

Evolution Timeline:
Week 1: Recognition
├ Identified protection mechanism
├ Noticed emotional triggers
└ Mapped intersection points

Week 2: Understanding
├ Explored pattern history
├ Identified benefits received
└ Acknowledged costs paid

Week 3: Experimentation
├ Small risk-taking
├ Pattern interruption
└ New response testing

Week 4: Integration
├ Pattern flexibility
├ Conscious choices
└ Balance finding
```

*Amanda's Implementation:* She dedicated a journal specifically to tracking this evolution. Each evening, she noted:

- Pattern manifestations
- Response experiments
- Results observed
- Insights gained

Her entry after one month revealed the power of pattern tracking:

*"Today, I noticed something remarkable. I could choose a different response when I consciously acknowledged my protection pattern. Instead of over-preparing in this morning's meeting, I allowed myself to speak from experience. The protection pattern is still there, but it's becoming more of a consultant than a commander."*

## PATTERN MATURITY INDICATORS

On a quiet Sunday morning, David spread his journals from the past six months across his office floor. He'd been tracking what he thought was a simple "fitness motivation" pattern, but the colored tabs marking different entries told a more complex story.

## PATTERN MATURITY ASSESSMENT TEMPLATE

```
Pattern: Fitness Motivation
Stage: Transitional

Maturity Indicators:
1. Awareness Level
   └ Recognition
      ├ Unconscious [Past]
      ├ Conscious [Current]
      └ Integrated [Goal]

2. Response Type
   └ Reaction
      ├ Automatic [Past]
      ├ Considered [Current]
      └ Chosen [Goal]

3. Flexibility
   └ Adaptation
      ├ Rigid [Past]
      ├ Experimenting [Current]
      └ Fluid [Goal]

4. Integration
   └ Embodiment
      ├ Disconnected [Past]
      ├ Connecting [Current]
      └ Unified [Goal]
```

David's Journal Entry: "May 15: Looking at my pattern's evolution is fascinating. Three months ago, missing a workout would trigger an all-or-nothing response—I'd abandon the entire week's routine. Now, I notice the urge to quit but can adjust instead. The pattern isn't just about exercise anymore; it's about how I handle commitment and flexibility in all areas."

## EXERCISE: PATTERN MATURITY MAPPING

1. Select an active pattern.
2. Assess current maturity level.

3. Track historical progression
4. Identify growth edges
5. Plan the next development stage.

## COMPLEX PATTERN RELATIONSHIPS

As David continued his analysis, he noticed how his fitness pattern connected to other life areas. He created a relationship map:

## PATTERN RELATIONSHIP MATRIX

```
Primary Pattern: Fitness Commitment

Related Patterns | Connection Type | Influence Direction | Impact Level
-----------------|-----------------|---------------------|------------
Work Discipline  | Reinforcing     | Bidirectional       | High
Sleep Habits     | Supporting      | Causal              | Medium
Social Calendar  | Competing       | Inverse             | High
Stress Response  | Triggering      | Reactive            | High
Food Choices     | Complementary   | Synergistic         | Medium
```

*David's Analysis Notes: "June 1: The connections are clearer now. Strong work discipline days usually mean a strong workout commitment. Poor sleep directly impacts next-day motivation. Social events often compete with workout times. High stress triggers either intense workouts or complete avoidance. Healthy eating naturally aligns with workout days."*

## PATTERN TRANSFORMATION POINTS

Through his analysis, David identified key points where pattern transformation was possible:

## TRANSFORMATION POINT TEMPLATE

```
Pattern State: Fitness Commitment
Current Level: Transitional

Key Transformation Points:
1. Decision Moments
   └ Morning Choice Points
      ├ Alarm response
      ├ Schedule review
      └ Energy check

2. Habit Anchors
   └ Existing Routines
      ├ Morning Coffee
      ├ Lunch break
      └ Evening wind-down

3. Environmental Triggers
   └ Space and Time
      ├ Gym bag visibility
      ├ Calendar blocks
      └ Workout space setup

4. Social Influences
   └ Support Systems
      ├ Workout partners
      ├ Class schedules
      └ Family expectations
```

*David's Implementation:* He began focusing on these transformation points, creating small experiments at each one. His journal captured the process:

*"June 15: Fascinating how small changes at key points affect the entire pattern. Moving my gym bag by the coffee maker meant seeing it during my strongest morning habit. Result: 80% morning workout completion this week versus 30% last month."*

Through this detailed examination, David's understanding of pattern transformation deepened. It wasn't about forcing change through willpower—it was about understanding and working with pattern relationships and transformation points.

# THREE
# COMPLEX PATTERN SYSTEMS

L auren leaned back in her chair, colored mind maps and journal entries scattered across her desk. Six months of tracking her "creativity blocks" had revealed something unexpected. She picked up an entry from March:

*"Another day staring at a blank canvas. Same paralysis, same fears. But wait—noticed something. It always happens after the client calls. After feedback sessions. After any external input..."*

## PATTERN WEB ANALYSIS

What Lauren had discovered wasn't a simple creativity block but a complex web of interconnected patterns. She created her first pattern web map:

## PATTERN WEB TEMPLATE

```
Central Theme: Creative Block

Level 1: Direct Patterns
├─ Time of Day
├─ Environment
├─ Energy Level
└─ Recent Inputs

Level 2: Contributing Patterns
├─ Client Interactions
├─ Self-Talk
├─ Perfectionism
└─ Risk Tolerance

Level 3: Root Patterns
├─ Validation Needs
├─ Identity Protection
├─ Professional Worth
└─ Artistic Expression

Connection Types:
↑ Reinforcing
↓ Diminishing
↔ Interacting
→ Triggering
```

*Lauren's Web Analysis Entry: "July 10: It's like discovering a spider's web in morning dew. Each strand connects to others, and vibrations in one area affect the whole. My creative blocks aren't random—they're part of an intricate protection system. External feedback triggers self-doubt, which activates perfectionism and paralyzes creativity. But seeing the web means I can finally work with it, not against it."*

## SHADOW PATTERNS

As Lauren dug deeper, she uncovered shadow patterns—unconscious influences operating beneath the surface:

## SHADOW PATTERN RECOGNITION TEMPLATE

```
Visible Pattern| Hidden Pattern  | Manifestation  | Impact | Trigger
---------------|--------------- -|----------------|--------|--------
Perfectionism  | Fear of Judgment| Procrastination| High   | Feedback
Block after    | Need for        | Avoiding       | High   | Client
client calls   | Control         | new projects   |        | Reviews
Creative       | Identity        | Over-planning  | Medium | Sharing
hesitation     | Protection      | sessions       |        | Work
```

## EXERCISE: SHADOW PATTERN DISCOVERY

1. Choose a persistent visible pattern.
2. List all manifestations.
3. Look for hidden drivers.
4. Identify triggers.
5. Map impacts.

*Lauren's Implementation:* She dedicated a full journal spread to mapping her shadow patterns, using different colors for each layer. Her notes revealed deeper insights:

*"July 15: The visible patterns are just the surface. Underneath my 'perfectionism' is a deep fear of judgment. Behind my 'creative blocks' is a protective instinct trying to preserve my artistic identity. These shadow patterns aren't enemies—they're trying to help, just in outdated ways."*

## GROWTH EDGE PATTERNS

Through her analysis, Lauren began identifying patterns that were ready for evolution—her growth edges:

## GOWTH EDGE MATRIX

| Pattern Area | Current State | Growth Signal | Next Level | Support Needed |
|---|---|---|---|---|
| Creative Process | Rigid | Frustration with rules | Flexible approach | Safe space to experiment |
| Client Response | Defensive | Awareness of reaction | Confident reception | Clear boundary and processes |
| Artistic Expression | Protected | Desire to share more | Authentic sharing | Supportive community |

*Lauren's Growth Edge Entry: "July 20: My growth edges speak to me. My frustration with my creative blocks is a signal—I'm ready for a more flexible approach. My defensiveness around feedback points to an emerging confidence that I want to be expressed. These aren't just problems to solve but invitations to evolve."*

## EXERCISE: GROWTH EDGE MAPPING

1. Identify patterns causing friction.
2. Note emotional responses.
3. Look for readiness signals.
4. Map desired evolution.
5. Plan support structures.

Lauren began transforming her creative blocks into stepping stones through this deep pattern work. Her final entry for the month revealed the power of understanding complex pattern systems:

*"July 31: Everything's connected—my creative blocks, my client interactions, and my artistic expression. Understanding the web of patterns allows me to work with the whole system rather than fight individual symptoms. When I honor the shadow patterns' protective intent while encouraging growth at the edges, something new emerges. My creativity isn't blocked; it's evolving."*

# FOUR
# ADVANCED RECOGNITION TECHNIQUES

Michael sat at his kitchen table early one morning, steam rising from his coffee cup. Before him lay three distinct journals: his work journal, personal journal, and pattern-tracking journal. For months, he'd been trying to understand why his leadership style shifted so dramatically under pressure.

## THE PATTERN MAPPING MATRIX

Reaching for a fresh page, Michael created his first multi-dimensional analysis:

## ADVANCED PATTERN MAPPING MATRIX

| Context Layer | Behavior Pattern | Emotional Pattern | Impact Pattern | Meta-Pattern |
|---------------|------------------|-------------------|----------------|--------------|
| High Pressure Meetings | Directive communication | Anxiety about outcomes | Team withdrawal | Control seeking |
| Regular Operations | Collaborative approach | Confident engagement | Team innovation | Trust building |
| Crisis Moments | Autocratic decisions | Fear of failure | Reduced initiative | Protection mode |

*Michael's Analysis Entry: "September 3: The matrix reveals something I've never seen before. My leadership isn't just changing—it's transforming through predictable stages. Each pressure point triggers a cascade: emotion → behavior → team impact. But seeing this cascade means I can interrupt it."*

## EXERCISE: CREATING YOUR PATTERN MATRIX

1. Choose three contexts
2. Map behaviors in each
3. Connect emotional states
4. Note impacts
5. Identify meta-patterns

## PATTERN INTERVENTION POINTS

Through his matrix analysis, Michael identified critical intervention points:

## INTERVENTION MAPPING TEMPLATE

```
Stage          | Early Signs    | Intervention      | Support         | Outcome
---------------|----------------|-------------------|-----------------|----------
Pre-Pressure   | Meeting        | Deep breathing    | Morning         | Maintained
               | scheduling     | practice          | preparation     | calm
               |                |                   |                 |
Initial        | Physical       | Pause and         | Team check-in   | Better
Tension        | tension        | ground            | protocol        | awareness
               |                |                   |                 |
Full Pattern   | Directive      | Switch to         | Trusted         | Pattern
Activation     | communication  | inquiry mode      | advisor         | interrupt
```

*Michael's Implementation:* He began carrying a small notebook for real-time pattern tracking:

*"September 10: Noticed tension rising in the budget meeting. Instead of jumping to directives, I paused for three breaths. I asked the team for input. A remarkable shift in energy—their innovative solutions emerged when I stepped back from control mode."*

## PATTERN TRANSFORMATION METHODS

Having identified his patterns and intervention points, Michael developed specific transformation techniques:

## PATTERN TRANSFORMATION TEMPLATE

```
Current Pattern: Pressure → Control → Team Withdrawal
Target Pattern: Pressure → Collaboration → Team Engagement

Transformation Steps:
1. Awareness
   └ Pattern Triggers
      ├ Time pressure
      ├ High stakes
      └ Uncertainty

2. Intervention
   .└ New Responses
      ├ Conscious pause
      ├ Team check-in
      └ Shared problem-solving

3. Practice
   └ Integration Methods
      ├ Daily reflection
      ├ Team feedback
      └ Success tracking

4. Reinforcement
   └ Support Systems
      ├ Leadership mentor
      ├ Team agreements
      └ Regular reviews
```

*Michael's Transformation Entry:* "*September 15: The old pattern tried to emerge in today's crisis meeting. Different this time. I caught it early and used the new protocol: pause, ground, and engage the team. Result: It was a better solution than I would have created alone, plus the team felt empowered. New pattern taking root.*"

## EXERCISE: PATTERN TRANSFORMATION PLANNING

1. Map current pattern
2. Design target pattern
3. Identify transformation steps

4. Create support structure

5. Track progress

Through this systematic approach, Michael wasn't just under-standing his leadership patterns—he was actively trans-forming them. His final entry for the month revealed the impact:

*"September 30: Leadership isn't about controlling outcomes; it's about creating spaces where the best outcomes can emerge. By understanding and transforming my patterns, I'm not just becoming a better leader—I'm helping my team become better leaders, too."*

# FIVE
# STRATEGIC APPLICATIONS

R achel opened her pattern tracking journal, a stack of Post-it notes marking significant insights from the past three months. As a senior product manager, she'd begun noticing how her decision-making patterns directly influenced project outcomes. Today, she was ready to use her pattern recognition skills strategically.

## DECISION-MAKING THROUGH PATTERN WISDOM

Rachel created her first Pattern-Based Decision Framework:

## DECISION PATTERN MATRIX

```
Decision Type | Pattern History | Current Triggers | Pattern Risk | Pattern Wisdom
------------- | --------------- | ---------------- | ------------ | ---------------
Quick         | Often reactive  | Time pressure    | Overlooking  | Pause for 2min
Operational   | under pressure  | Team stress      | alternatives | pattern check
              |                 |                  |              |
Strategic     | Best after      | Stakeholder      | Analysis     | Create space
Planning      | reflection      | expectations     | paralysis    | for emergence
              |                 |                  |              |
Team          | Most effective  | Competing        | Defaulting to| Include multi-
Alignment     | with input      | priorities       | authority    | pattern view
```

*Rachel's Decision Journal Entry: "October 5: Fascinating how awareness of decision patterns changes everything. In today's product review, instead of rushing to solutions, I noticed the familiar pressure pattern emerging. Paused. I asked what patterns we'd seen in similar decisions. The team's collective pattern wisdom led to a breakthrough approach we'd have missed in reactive mode."*

## EXERCISE: DECISION PATTERN MAPPING

1. List recent key decisions
2. Identify patterns in the approach
3. Note outcomes and insights
4. Map pattern influences
5. Create wisdom guidelines

## FUTURE PATTERN PROJECTION

Rachel developed a system for projecting pattern implications into future scenarios:

## PATTERN PROJECTION TEMPLATE

| Current Pattern | Future Context | Likely Evolution | Desired Outcome | Bridge Steps |
|---|---|---|---|---|
| Team collaboration | Remote-first transition | Communication gaps growing | Strengthened connections | 1. Virtual rituals |
| Innovation approach | Market uncertainty | Risk-averse decisions | Balanced risk taking | 1. Safe-fail experiments |
| Leadership style | Company growth | Increased control needs | Adaptive leadership | 1. Pattern awareness |

*Rachel's Projection Notes: "October 12: By projecting current patterns forward, we can see potential challenges before they emerge. Our collaboration pattern that works now will need intentional evolution for remote work. Starting small experiments today to develop new patterns for tomorrow."*

## LIFE DESIGN THROUGH PATTERN UNDERSTANDING

Rachel began applying pattern wisdom to intentional life design:

## PATTERN-BASED LIFE DESIGN FRAMEWORK

```
Life Area     | Current Pattern| Desired Pattern  | Design Elements | Integration
--------------|----------------|------------------|-----------------|------------
Professional  | Reactive       | Strategic        | Morning         | Weekly
Growth        | learning       | development      | study ritual    | review
              |                |                  |                 |
Work-Life     | Boundary       | Fluid            | Technology      | Daily
Balance       | blurring       | integration      | boundaries      | shutdown
              |                |                  |                 |
Creative      | Sporadic       | Consistent       | Creative        | Project
Expression    | engagement     | practice         | scheduling      | rhythm
```

## EXERCISE: LIFE DESIGN MAPPING

1. Select key life areas
2. Map current patterns
3. Envision desired patterns
4. Design support structures
5. Create integration plan

*Rachel's Design Journey: "October 20: Understanding my patterns has transformed how I design my life. Instead of forcing changes, I'm learning to work with natural pattern flows. I noticed my best creative work follows deep strategic thinking. Now intentionally scheduling strategy sessions before creative blocks."*

She created a daily pattern check-in practice:

## MORNING PATTERN REVIEW:

1. Which patterns were served yesterday?
2. What patterns might emerge today?
3. Where are pattern opportunities?
4. What pattern support is needed?

*Final October Entry: "October 31: Pattern recognition isn't just a tool anymore—it's becoming a way of seeing and creating. Each day brings new pattern insights, not just about what is but about what could be. By understanding the patterns that shape our reality, we gain the wisdom to shape new possibilities."*

# SIX
# INTEGRATION AND MASTERY

Katherine sat in her study, surrounded by a year's worth of pattern journals. Colored threads connected different entries across her desk, creating a physical web of her pattern journey. She picked up her latest journal, ready to document her path to pattern mastery.

## DAILY PATTERN PRACTICE TEMPLATE

```
Time of Day     | Practice Focus | Integration Tool | Outcome Measure
----------------|----------------|------------------|----------------
Morning         | Pattern        | Awareness        | Pattern
(6:30-7:00)     | Scanning       | Checklist        | Recognition
                |                |                  |
Midday          | Pattern        | Response         | Pattern
(12:30-1:00)    | Response       | Tracking         | Navigation
                |                |                  |
Evening         | Pattern        | Reflection       | Pattern
(9:00-9:30)     | Integration    | Journal          | Learning
```

*Katherine's Practice Entry: "November 3: This morning's pattern scan revealed something subtle. My resistance to early meetings isn't about the timing—it's about preparation anxiety. By catching this pattern early, I could work with it rather than push against it. Set prep time the night before transformed the entire experience."*

## EXERCISE: BUILDING YOUR PRACTICE

1. Choose consistent times
2. Create environment supports
3. Develop review rituals
4. Track effectiveness
5. Adjust as needed

## TOOLS FOR ADVANCED PRACTICE

Katherine developed a comprehensive toolkit for pattern mastery:

## PATTERN MASTERY TOOLKIT

```
Tool Type          | Purpose             | Application         | Integration
-------------------|---------------------|---------------------|--------------
Pattern            | Capture emerging    | Quick-note          | Daily review
Journal            | insights            | system              | practice
                   |                     |                     |
Pattern            | Track pattern       | Digital             | Weekly
Tracker            | frequencies         | tracking app        | analysis
```

*Katherine's Tool Notes: "November 10: Each tool serves a specific purpose in pattern mastery. The quick-capture journal catches insights in the moment. The tracker helps identify frequencies. Maps reveal relationships. The portfolio shows the journey. Together, they create a complete system for pattern understanding and transformation."*

## MOVING FORWARD

As her practice deepened, Katherine created a framework for ongoing pattern mastery:

## PATTERN MASTERY FRAMEWORK

| Level of Mastery | Key Indicators | Growth Areas | Next Steps |
|------------------|----------------|--------------|------------|
| Pattern Recognition | - Quick recognition<br>- Basic mapping | - Deeper pattern subtleties<br>- Complex relationships | - Advanced scanning practice |
| Pattern Response | - Effective interventions<br>- Clear outcomes | - Pattern prediction<br>- Proactive adjustment | - Response refinement exercises |
| Pattern Integration | - Natural integration<br>- Intuitive navigation | - Teaching others<br>- System creation | - Mastery projects<br>- Community building |

*Katherine's Integration Entry: "November 15: Pattern mastery isn't a destination—it's an evolving journey. Each level brings new insights, challenges, and opportunities. The key is maintaining beginners' curiosity while building advanced skills."*

## EXERCISE: MASTERY MAPPING

1. Assess current level
2. Identify growth edges
3. Plan the next development steps
4. Create support structures
5. Track progress

*Katherine's Final Entry: "November 30: Looking back over this year of pattern work, I see how far this practice has come. What started as simple pattern recognition has evolved into a comprehensive life practice. Patterns aren't just something I study anymore—they're a lens through which I understand and create my life.*

*Each day brings new pattern discoveries. Each challenge offers pattern wisdom. Each success builds pattern mastery. This isn't just about seeing patterns—it's about dancing with them, growing through them, creating with them.*

*The journey continues, but now with a deeper understanding and greater purpose. Here's to the patterns yet to be discovered, the wisdom yet to be gained, and the transformations yet to unfold."*

## CONCLUSION

As we close this guide to Advanced Pattern Recognition, remember that mastery is not about perfection—it's about presence, practice, and continuous evolution. Your pattern journey is unique to you. Trust it, explore it, and let it unfold in its own perfect pattern.